EASY-BAKE OVEN

Jessica Rusick

Big Buddy Books

An Imprint of Abdo Publishing
abdobooks.com

abdobooks.com

Published by Abdo Publishing, a division of ABDO, PO Box 398166, Minneapolis, Minnesota 55439. Copyright © 2022 by Abdo Consulting Group, Inc. International copyrights reserved in all countries. No part of this book may be reproduced in any form without written permission from the publisher. Big Buddy Books™ is a trademark and logo of Abdo Publishing.

Printed in the United States of America, North Mankato, Minnesota
102021
012022

THIS BOOK CONTAINS
RECYCLED MATERIALS

Design: Emily O'Malley, Mighty Media, Inc.
Production: Mighty Media, Inc.
Editor: Liz Salzmann
Cover Photographs: Bradross63/Wikimedia Commons (old oven), Mighty Media, Inc. (Ronald Howes, blue oven), RuthBlack/iStockphoto (cupcakes), Shannon/Flickr (Oreo mix), SherSor/Shutterstock Images (chocolate cake)
Interior Photographs: Allen/Flickr, p. 17; Carol M. Highsmith Archive/Library of Congress, p. 27; Charles Sykes/AP Images, pp. 25, 29 (right); Chris Willson/Alamy Photo, pp. 13, 28 (top); EQRoy/Shutterstock Images, pp. 7, 28 (bottom); Evan Long/Flickr, pp. 11, 29 (left); Kevin Winter/Getty Images, p. 21; Mighty Media, Inc., pp. 15, 29 (bottom); mikdam/iStockphoto, p. 9; Pearls of Jannah/Flickr, p. 19; RBerteig/Flickr, p. 23; Wholtone/Wikimedia Commons, p. 5

Library of Congress Control Number: 2021942805

Publisher's Cataloging-in-Publication Data
Names: Rusick, Jessica, author.
Title: Easy-bake oven: Ronald Howes / by Jessica Rusick
Description: Minneapolis, Minnesota : Abdo Publishing, 2022 | Series: Toy stories | Includes online resources and index.
Identifiers: ISBN 9781532197109 (lib. bdg.) | ISBN 9781098219239 (ebook)
Subjects: LCSH: Inventors--Juvenile literature. | Halogen oven cooking--Juvenile literature. | Toys--Juvenile literature. | Baking--Juvenile literature. | Hasbro Entertainment (Firm)--Juvenile literature.
Classification: DDC 338.47688--dc23

CONTENTS

CHAPTER 1

RONALD HOWES

Ronald Bruce Howes was born on May 22, 1926. His parents were Elizabeth White and Emerson Clarence Howes. Ronald's mother died when he was a baby. He was raised by his grandmother in Cincinnati, Ohio. Ronald's family ran several small grocery stores there.

Ronald grew up in Cincinnati's Over-the-Rhine neighborhood. This area is known for its historic buildings.

CHAPTER 2

SCHOOL & WAR

Ronald was a smart child. He taught himself to read before kindergarten! Later, Ronald went to Walnut Hills High School in Cincinnati. He also took classes at the University of Cincinnati.

In the 1940s, Ronald fought in **World War II** for two years. He then returned to Ohio. He earned an **engineering degree** at the University of Cincinnati.

The University of Cincinnati was established in 1870. Its engineering program is one of the best in the nation.

 BRIGHT IDEA

After graduating, Howes worked for toy company Kenner Products. He helped invent new toys.

In the early 1960s, Kenner salesman Norman Shapiro saw pretzel sellers in New York City. This gave him an idea for a new toy. Shapiro thought Kenner should make a pretzel oven for kids. Howes loved this idea!

Food vendors have sold soft pretzels in New York City since the early 1800s.

DEVELOPING THE OVEN

Howes and his coworkers **developed** Shapiro's idea. The team decided to make an oven for kids. It would cook small cakes, cookies, and more.

The oven would use lightbulbs to cook food. Howes worked to create baking mixes for the oven. He tested them at his house.

Many Easy-Bake Oven mixes come with frosting and sprinkles.

EASY-BAKE DEBUT

The Easy-Bake Oven **debuted** in 1963. It came with small pans, bowls, and other cooking supplies. It also came with 12 baking mixes. The food was baked in a small oven **chamber**. Kids could watch the food cook through a tiny window.

The first Easy-Bake Oven came in both yellow and turquoise.

The Easy-Bake Oven was a hit. It sold 500,000 in its first year! Also in 1963, Howes married Nancy Lee. The two had met at Kenner. Howes and Nancy went on to have six children.

Howes worked on many other toys at Kenner.
One was a drawing toy called a Spirograph.

A simple and fascinating way to DRAW a million marvelous patterns
Kenner's NEW SPIROGRAPH
For all ages... Anyone can draw beautiful patterns immediately!
Create your own and use the SPIROGRAPH Booklet
No limit to the different designs you can make!
WINNER OF THE EDUCATIONAL TOY OF THE YEAR AWARD U.S.A.
WINNER OF DESIGN IDEA OF THE MONTH DESIGN NEWS U.S.A.
WINNER OF ARTISTIC TOY OSCAR PARIS
SPIROGRAPH SET contains:
18 Transparent Plastic Wheels
2 Transparent Plastic Rings
2 Transparent Plastic Racks
4 Ball point Pens
Red, Blue, Green, Black
Baseboard and Pack of Paper
Fitted Storage Tray for
Wheels, Rings, Racks, Pins and Pens
16-page full-color illustrated
Pattern Booklet with easy instructions.
Perfect "mesh" of the wheels, rings and racks. You
hold the pen yourself and actually draw the pattern.
SPIROGRAPH

BRAND-NEW BAKING

By 1967, more than 2 million Easy-Bake Ovens had been sold. The same year, food company General Mills bought Kenner. General Mills owned the popular Betty Crocker cake mix **brand**. Soon, young bakers could bake **miniature** Betty Crocker cakes!

Betty Crocker Easy-Bake mixes could be baked in Easy-Bake Ovens or regular ovens.

CHAPTER 7

MICROWAVE MEALS

Kenner and General Mills **released** new Easy-Bake Oven models over the next years. By the 1980s, microwave ovens were popular in the United States. So, new Easy-Bake Ovens looked like microwave ovens! New mixes and **accessories** let kids cook pizza, potato chips, and more.

Since 1973, Easy-Bake Ovens
have included a pan pusher.
This tool allows users to safely
push pans into the oven.

CHAPTER 8

REAL MEAL OVEN

In 1991, toy company Hasbro bought Kenner. The company **redesigned** the Easy-Bake Oven several times.

In 2003, Hasbro **released** the Easy-Bake Real Meal Oven. This was the first Easy-Bake Oven to cook without a lightbulb. Instead, electricity heated a metal part inside the oven.

In 2003, Olia Wall (*right*) won Hasbro's Easy-Bake Baker of the Year contest. She got to bake with Jay Leno (*left*) on *The Tonight Show*.

CHAPTER 9

HALL OF FAME

By 2006, more than 23 million Easy-Bake Ovens had been sold. That year, the Easy-Bake Oven entered the National Toy Hall of Fame.

Also in 2006, Hasbro **redesigned** the Easy-Bake Oven again. Unfortunately, the oven had a safety problem. So, Hasbro had to **recall** it. But Hasbro fixed the problem for the next model.

The 2006 Easy-Bake Oven (*pictured*) was recalled because some children got their fingers stuck in the front opening.

CHAPTER 10

LASTING LEGACY

Ronald Howes died on February 16, 2010. He was 83 years old. Howes was remembered for his work on the Easy-Bake Oven. The next year, Hasbro **redesigned** the toy again. The Easy-Bake **Ultimate** Oven looked modern. It also had a larger cooking **chamber**.

Hasbro used gender-neutral colors for the Easy-Bake Ultimate Oven. It came in black or purple.
Easy-Bake Ultimate Oven
DANGER: TO PREVENT ELECTRIC SHOCK DO NOT IMMERSE IN WATER. WIPE CLEAN WITH A DAMP CLOTH.
CAUTION - ELECTRIC TOY: This toy has a heating element which can result in burns. Not recommended for children under 8 years of age. As with all electric products, precautions should be observed during handling and use to prevent electric shock.
CAUTION - SUPERVISION REQUIRED - ELECTRIC TOY

In 2013, the Easy-Bake Oven had its fiftieth **anniversary**. On November 4, 2017, **historian** Todd Coopee started National Easy-Bake Oven Day. It is a day to celebrate the toy's history. The Easy-Bake Oven would be remembered as a toy loved by millions of children.

In 2016, Cincinnati artist Jonathan Queen created a mural featuring the Easy-Bake Oven and other Kenner toys.

TIMELINE

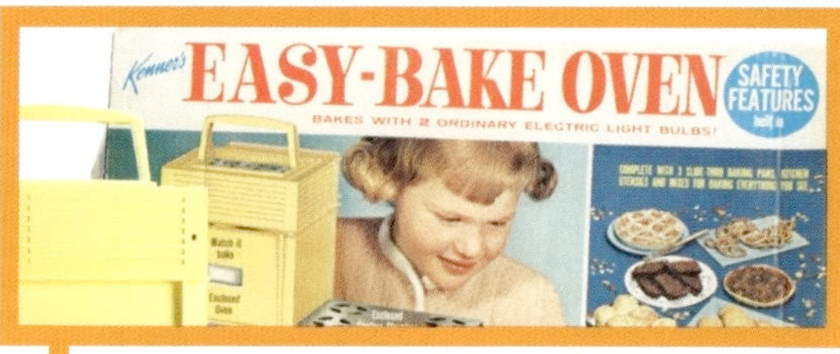

1926
Ronald Bruce Howes is born on May 22.

1963
The Easy-Bake Oven debuts. Howes marries Nancy Lee.

2003
Hasbro releases the Easy-Bake Real Meal Oven.

1940s
Howes earns a degree in engineering from the University of Cincinnati.

1967
General Mills buys Kenner Products. More than 2 million Easy-Bake Ovens have been sold.

2006

The Easy-Bake Oven enters the National Toy Hall of Fame. More than 23 million ovens have been sold since 1963.

2011

Hasbro releases the Easy-Bake Ultimate Oven.

2010

Howes dies on February 16.

2017

National Easy-Bake Oven Day is started by historian Todd Coopee.

GLOSSARY

accessory—something that is not necessary but makes something else more useful, attractive, or effective.

anniversary—the date of a special event that is often celebrated each year.

brand—a category of products made by a particular company and all having the same company name.

chamber—an enclosed space or section.

debut (DAY-byoo)—to make a first appearance.

degree—a title given by a college, university, or trade school to its students for completing their studies.

develop—to create something over time.

engineering (ehn-juh-NIHR-ihng)—applying scientific knowledge to a practical purpose such as building machines or buildings.

historian—a person who studies or writes about history.

miniature (MIH-nee-uh-chur)—a smaller version of something else.

recall—when a company asks people to return a product that has a problem or is dangerous.

redesign—to create a new or better version of something.

release—to make available to the public.

ultimate—the best or greatest.

World War II—a war fought in Europe, Asia, and Africa from 1939 to 1945.

INDEX